CW00531149

# *The Silent Voice*

## An Anthology of Poetry

### Edited By Amanda Read

δ

Published by Dogma Publications

Dogma Publications Bicester Innovation Centre, Telford Road
Bicester, Oxon OX26 4LD England

**The Silent Voice**

Cover picture taken from Anthonie van Borssum's
*Extensive River View with a Horseman*
1660s
Museum of Fine Arts, Budapest

First Published 2005
by Dogma Publications

ISBN 1-84591-009-5

Printed in Great Britain for Dogma Publications

# *The Silent Voice*

# Contents

# Contents Continued

# Contents Continued

**The Silent Voice**

His festering silence surged from within
Silent screams formed by sin
The torrent raging deep inside
Brimmed then flooded heaving tide

Crushing pain inward borne
Tore the heart left human form
Agonies wrestled mind and soul
No longer kept his body whole

His torturing jailor now no more
Captive spirit settled the score
Head gave hand monsters might
Ripped through dark to search for light

Child now man released to peace
Endless cries gave him release
Tortured spirit blighted life
Demon heart now pierced with knife

Black heart shell held life no more
Lifeless mass streaked red the floor
Crushed spirit freed unleashed from stain
Innocuous stream washed free the shame

**Sally Richards**

## No Hand

No hand to close the window
No hand to shut the doors
The windows and doors are open wide
Your secrets are out, and flying about
Don't try to catch them but let them be free
Just like me, just like me.

**Marilyn Knott**

## Forest Winter

Winter creaks oaks of old
Winter's bleak, so cold, so cold
Frost cracks and stills the river bed
Snowdrop lifts its fragile head

Winter leaches colours bold
Winter's bitter, like stone, like stone
Leaves crisp and shatter silenced air
Morning mist o'er fields bare

Winter bites life to fold
Winter's dank, like mould, like mould
Mice hunt and forage summer invest
Wren and robin tend their nest

Breath of winter unforgiving and long
Dormant forest dreams of sun.

**Jayne E Dawson**

## One Must Go

One must go
And one must stay
It is the way of life
But we have the memory
Of our husband or our wife.

The courtship, the marriage
And then the honeymoon
The thrill or our creation
Of our very first new home.

Then comes the darling baby
In its tiny cot and carriage
A little gent or lady
The completion of the marriage.

But one must go
And one must stay
If happens every day
But we have the golden memories
To help us on our way.

**Ida Pressley**

## The World With Total Silence From Humans

The world with total silence from humans,
Could make the world a better place in many ways.
A parent could not tell off their children,
For not clearing up their room for days.

There would be much more quiet for teachers,
When there is trouble no need to shout.
No need to teach kids grammar or math sums,
There would be no talking, loud kids about.

There would be no laws or age restrictions,
We could do what we wanted when we pleased.
There would be no bossy boots around,
And no horrible people who often tease.

There would be no annoying entertainment,
There would be no start to horrible war.
No quarrelling, shouting or swearing,
No crying when our bodies are sore.

The world with total silence from humans,
Would make the world a better place in many ways.
But let's think about this properly,
Would it be a better place to spend our days?

How could we talk about our problems?
How could we sing, dance or play?
How could we share our love with others?
How could we talk about our day?

How could we communicate on the phone?
How could we laugh and show others that we care?
The world would be absolutely nothing in silence,
Human emotions are a pleasure to share!

**Jessica Carmody**

## Birthday Blues

Tomorrow is my birthday; I'm feeling rather low.
Yes, tomorrow is the day when I hit that big six O
I do not feel like sixty, except for early morn.
I no more feel like sixty than the day when I was born.
I gaze into my mirror; all the evidence is there,
The crows feet round my eyeballs, the grey streaks in me hair.
I still fancy all the film stars, Brad Pitt and Leonardo,
The only blokes who ask me out are toothless desperados.
Twenty was a great age, the start of adult hood.
Thirty I could cope with, I still felt and looked real good.
At forty things began to sag, my self-esteem dipped badly.
At fifty I was real depressed till I went on HRT.
A new lease of life that gave me, I went dancing, I went clubbing,
But tomorrow I'll be sixty and I really can't help blubbing.

I'll go and collect me pension, me prescriptions will all be free.
I'll ride on the buses for half price, that's no consolation for me.
But wait. With this extra money I could get me saggy bits shifted.
Me figure would be so much better
With me boobs and me bum uplifted.
If I put some red streaks in me hair, and maybe a stud here and there,
With a top really low and jeans cut really tight,
Some six inch stilettos, all shiny and bright,
Should I get a tattoo? No, don't want to look tarty,
Just cause a sensation at me own birthday party.
Then go out on the pull and find a young man,
A handsome strong toy boy, all muscles and tan,
If a girl's only as old as the bloke that she woos,
By this time next week I could be twenty two.

**Laurie Elgar**

## Domestic Violence

I wonder what happened to the Geoff I once knew
Who could be as gentle as the morning dew?
If only he could piece together the clues
He might prevent himself from sinking into a murky stew
Making a place with no visitors and no views
His work it is devouring him
Which could be rated a sort of sin
Personality, losing its glow and becoming dim
For Geoff is Geoff no more
I worry for what his future, may have in store
He is a man with a new exterior
Who thinks others inferior?
What destroys me most is the inner change
Which causes him on occasions to become deranged
For Geoff is Geoff no more
His violent outbursts rearing
Their heads like crippled cranes
Thus rendering me more pain
For Geoff is Geoff no more
Who does not rate his original score?
It is difficult for me to describe what he's become
The future for us glum
His life I have already saved twice
Mine he could throw away at the toss of a dice
He could walk away and let me die
Believe me it's no lie
For Geoff is Geoff no more.

**Molly Warren**

## I Wish To Be Your Wish

I wish to be your wish,
So I can fill your every desire,
For when I look at you,
My eyes burn, like fire.

I give you a wish,
Make it last forever,
Lets both try this,
Let us be together.

A wish is for you,
A wish is for me,
A wish for us both,
A wish to my heart for you are the key.

I used my wish,
I wished to be yours,
You have your wish,
Make me happy, my life no flaws.

A wish is yours,
A wish for free,
My only wish,
Is for yours to be me.

So come make your wish,
I'll make it come true,
All that I'm saying,
Is that I love you.

**David Salomon**

## The Oak

The oak stands firm and strong,
It lives for very long,
Leaves fall,
Oak stands tall,
Never doing a wrong.

So it stands all the years,
Hearing so many fears,
Its protected and shown,
Tattered and blown,
The sap its amber tears.

But the oak is long gone,
Though still lived for very long,
The soul now dead,
At life it said,
'The earth shall hear my song'.

**Karla Tyson Berglund**

## The Crooked Oak

There was an oak from way back,
That twisted and curved like a switch back.
It was as a child playing with my brother,
When we ran across the scented fields of clover.

In the corner was our haven,
Where we would climb up into heaven.
And from the top survey our world,
The winding river, glistening like a pearl.

The leaning willows observe their reflection,
The passing swans in their regal perfection,
For a few hours we are king of all we see,
Until our rumbling stomachs tell us it's time for tea!

I wonder now as an old lady, is that tree still there and the cows,
Are there other children climbing to a welcome in her boughs?
Oh I would that I could return to those idyllic years.
To remember all the fun we had brings me close to tears.

**Ann Penn**

## My Son

Look at his eyes
See how they shine so bright
You know they always shined for me
But I look back and I find
Just what I left behind
And I find I was too blind to see
That the chances I've had
To make good what was bad
Have suddenly all passed me by
And as I look through this book
Of the photos you took
I remember again and I cry
No one can deny
In the blink of an eye
My son, he was taken from me
And no one can say why
My son had to die
Just one of those things that must be
I now know what I lack
It's the love I hold back
And I never showed love when I could
I'll go back if I may
And relive every day
And give back all the love that I should
And at nighttime I find
Just what he left behind?
For his eyes they still sparkle and shine
And when my son he did die
A star shines in the sky
So I can find him when I die.

**Anthony Redden**

**The Princess And The Star**
*(written for Ella aged 7 years)*

The lovely Princess Ella lived in a magic land,
In a castle made of chocolate, by blue sea and golden sand.
A little bridge of spiders' webs, stretched across the shore,
Threads of gold and silver, reached up to her door.

Her friends were fish and dolphins, who came to play each day;
Seahorses would wave to her as they rode upon the spray.
Fairies from the magic wood, quite often called her name;
'Hello there, Princess Ella, please come and join our game'.

Princess Ella loved her friends, but her favourite was by far,
When the day turned into night, a big bright shining star.
Glow-worms lit a staircase, reaching way up high,
Moonbeams danced before her, as she climbed up to the sky.

Together they would hide and seek, play hopscotch on the moon,
Race to Mars and Jupiter; morning always came too soon.
The days were filled with laughter, but she never strayed too far,
As when the sun had gone to bed, there waiting was her star.

**Joyce M Lord**

## Just A Wish

The dawn broke through the mist filled sky
as I lay awake in my bed.
A Skylark sang his merry song.
true promise of a warm day ahead.

If I had a wish my wish would be.
To live in a world where everyone's free
Where all could be happy, and famine be gone
With all of my heart that's what I long.

Where the rich and the poor would live as one.
With none of the talk of who's better than some.
Where born of a woman and breath the same air
So lets beg forgiveness and try to be fair.

**Heather Subryan**

## Oz...A Tribute To A Friend

Quiet in his basket lying, sleeping the sleep that transcends time.
The struggle of the night has ended by moving to a rest, sublime
He'd been our friend for sixteen years; he'd brightened up the days,
of lives that oft times were mundane, with quiet, pleasing ways,
We find it hard as we reflect of many years passed by,
to imagine days before he came, no matter how we try
But come he did, as if by chance, a happening unplanned,
but are these things just left to luck or guided by fates hand?
Our home was then replete with pets;
he had to find his place, he managed this with dignity,
No anger on the face, of other dogs
and veteran mogs who took to him with grace,
A pup whose unassuming ways engendered trust in one and all,
in humans or in animals it wasn't hard to fall
For this small even tempered dog who seldom showed aggression
and yet he could assert himself if ever intercession
Was necessary to defend his home, his charges, or his friends,
he'd rid the barn of plagues of rats attacking helpless hens
And yet when puppy Rosie came and later Mrs. Mop,
he cared for them with tenderness, his patience never stopped.
Mrs. Mop a rescue dog, an inmate of the home
He took her from the Spartan cage in which she lived alone
Rosie was his sole mate, together they grew old and tho' 'girl dog'
was twice his size with him she wasn't bold
The only time his cool was shaken was when young Maxwell came;
a JRT, short fuse, small brain, he really took the blame
for all the squabbles, fracas, spats
that involved them both in fierce combat,
Until a common danger posed, they worked together fighting foes
and when that current danger past
they resumed their spatting to the last
And now he's gone I've dug his grave the flowers grow on top,
the sorrow fades, the pain will dull, but memories will never stop.

**John Harrison**

## Getting Old

Remember when you were young
You use to dance and you had fun
But now you're getting old
You just will not be told.

You can't do this you can't do that
Your creaking bones will set you back
Try and dance if you dare
You'll end up sitting on the chair.

But if you're brave and have a go
Of yourself you'll make a show
Just go wild and have a jig
But don't go home without your wig.

If you drink then take it easy
If you don't you'll feel queasy
When your old and off your head
It might be wise to stay in bed.

**Betty Coleborn**

**My Magic Hat**

A bully came up to me
As I was climbing down a bookshelf.
He clenched his fist, and stamped his foot,
And I nearly wet myself.

As I thought of what to do,
I realised my magic hat.
And took it of with a little grab,
And I gave it a silent pat.

Suddenly a whirlwind flew around the bully,
It made him weep and cry.
All the teachers came to see,
That a little boy could fly.

I quickly put my head in a book,
So nobody would see
At the end of the day as I said goodbye
To all the teachers
They never knew it was me!

**Heather Dunlop**

**Summer Blazing**
*(A rising field of Rape seen from the roadside)*

Saffron covered hillside,
Like a yellow sail,
Ruffled by a catspaw,
Piping up a gale.

Primrose yellow hillside
Like a living beast,
Bare boned trees on skyline,
Cloud pennants streaming east.

Sunflower yellow hillside,
Yellow of a golden hue,
Vibrant, breathing, elemental,
Surely, Vincent coloured you.

**W H Billington**

## Forbidden Fruit

I've waited all my life it seems,
To know a love like this;
Gay abandoned passion,
The thrill of our first kiss.
I don't know how it happened,
I don't know if I knew;
That you were meant for me,
As much, as I was meant for you.
I try to analyse our love,
But find no answers there;
Why can't I just accept our fate,
Enjoy our love affair.
This maybe just a fleeting thing,
Our crazy wild romance;
But love like this comes round but once;
I think I'll take a chance.

**Sue Fellows**

## Sadistic Pleasure

Tally-Ho, Tally-Ho
Its fun sirs, its fun
Hounds at the ready
And the fox on the run.

Tally-Ho, Tally-Ho
With drinks all round
Off at a gallop
Before the fox goes to ground.

Tally-Ho, its fun sirs,
Jumping hedge, ditch and gate
Seeing the poor creature
Eluding its fate.

Tally-Ho, Tally-Ho
How can it be fun?
The fox ripped apart
It's brush you have won.

Tally-Ho, Tally-Ho
Its fun sirs, just a game
Let the tables be turned sirs
To feel terror and pain.

**Jenny L Treacher**

## The Marionette
*(written when my  Parkinson's Disease got worse)*

As I wake my body tenses
with feline stealth I stretch my limbs.
Dragged too soon from the arms of Morpheus,
I submit to my Master's whims.
He holds the strings, controls my movements,
with cruel jerks I turn and fall - childlike I inch and shuffle slowly
leaning against the wall.
An hour passes, now it's time to curl my toes around the rope.
I am not shown how far it reaches but step firmly, full of hope.
The Puppeteer, for his amusement,
lets my guiding reins go slack - panic,
terror overcome me - take a deep breath and relax.,
Tension shows in all my muscles, knotted like a puppet's strings,
shoulders hunched and eyeballs sunken, how I wish for angels' wings.
Once my step was light and nimble, nothing was too much for me,
now I cross a tightrope daily, just to reach normality.

**Sue Moore**

## Buzz Off

The fly in the room is buzzing around
It gets on my nerves makes a horrible sound
Can't seem to think or concentrate
It's now become a figure of hate.

I open the window it doesn't fly out
It looks like it will, then turns about
I'm sure it does it just to annoy
Now I've decided it must be destroyed.

With swatter in hand I follow it round
I give it a clout it falls to the ground
As I go to throw him out the door
He flies back inside along with two more.

**John Wallbridge**

## I Have Been Blest

I have been blest to see you, Poetry.
For I have seen you in the fields and hills
And watched you in the blue-green ocean's folds
For there you hide yourself.
I am so blest to see you, Poetry.

I have been blest that I have heard your song
In wind-whipped branches dancing in the breeze
And heard you in the sighing of the wind
And songs of blackbirds warbling in the trees.
I have been blest to hear you, Poetry
But I have seen you too, in children's eyes
And heard you in their laughter;
And, surely, in the heart of every flower
And in the rippling of every stream
You can be found; if we have eyes to see
And ears to hear, we'll find you, Poetry.

**Mary Hunt**

## First Ice

Young tears flow
Like liquid stalactites
Streaming like a banner
Cold and bitter, as the phone falls from her hand
Dressed for splendour
In earrings and dress
But alone, alone, alone and distraught
Scarred with the spirit of human malice
A first taste of venom
And a first taste of remorse, repent and regret
Dragging her demoralised soul
Along the rain laden street
Past the frost-mantled walls of the alleys
The first ice of the winter heart
The ice of the once warm feelings
Now frozen heart
Of reject and disappointment
Slowly, slowly asphyxiating,
In the first ice of a broken heart

**Callan J Davies**

**Our Last Goodbye**

With heads bowed low
We trudged across the rain soaked field
The lightening flash and thunder roll heralding
The finality of our parting deed
Alone with our private thoughts of you
But now united as one in our grief

No cold, hard slab for your final resting place
In sombre churchyard grave
But sun warmed weathered rocks
Where you once found solitude and peace
As you gazed at the river
Tumbling past you to the sea

As we stood at the river's edge
Our tears mingled with the falling rain
Clutching each other for emotional support
Staring with unseeing eyes at the scene around us
Our hearts must surely break
With the unbearable pain of our last goodbye

But when we released you in the water
Oh how you soared!
Twisting, turning, sinking, floating
In a glorious golden sunlit starburst
At last we had set you free
And with you went some of our pain

Goodbye sweet spirit, fly to eternity

**Catherine Rust**

## On Harrow-on-the-Hill

Something I thought
Would never happen *happened*:
I thought of the hill
Without thinking of you:

I remembered the trains, long lines of light,
And Ruislip through the trees;
Reading gravestones by torchlight;
And dry grass scratching in the breeze.

I saw the church's red-tipped spire;
And the steep road down to South Harrow;
The Castle with its open fire;
And queuing planes above Heathrow.

The cranes of Uxbridge to the North;
And, east: The Weald, and Wealdstone,
To Rayner's Lane, and Rickmansworth.
And, west: Park Royal, and Alperton.

I thought of Eddie, of George, and Rob,
Of Jim, and Ian, and Bob;
Of Claire, and Kelly, even Banu;
But never once of you.

Something I thought
Would never happen, *happened*:
I thought of the hill
Without thinking of you.

**Joel Saggers**

## Transparency

You could swallow me whole if I
wasn't so sharp.
Drink me in 'til you're giddy with
fright.
Hold me up to the
stars
Like a smeary glass.

Lick a finger and run it
round my rim.
Turn me to the tune of my flaws
and chew over what you hear.

Let me slip
                 Listen - fallen silence.

**Laura Paton**

## Oblivion

I stumble, aimlessly wandering through the chaos of my life,
Surveying the carnage my selfishness has wrought.
I trip upon the image of you, shattered into a billion pieces,
Each one piercing my wretched, naked feet.
And yet, I walk on, to destinations unknown,
My tattered robes billowing in the unforgiving gale
Which howls and howls and howls,
Screaming its taunts into my ears,
Whipping up the crumbled shards of perception
To blast them in my eyes.

These things I deserve.
The ruinous nature of my obsession is clear.
I deserve these things.

I clutch at a shred of sanity and devour it greedily.
I must work out what to do
To smooth over the treacherous waters of my own making;
The storm brewing ominously in my brain
Must be kept at bay.

Oh God, I feel I must go mad.
Every synapse filling with dread,
Freezing with fear,
Cracking with the enormity of what I have done.

Oh God, what have I done?
Oh God, what must I do?

**Jonathan Ralph**

## Change Life

Our world has become so divided
Nobody talks anymore
Whites only mix with whites
And blacks stick with their own
I'm trying to teach my children
It's braver to just walk away.

I try to teach my children
To treat everyone the same
But what's the point in me
Teaching them
When the worlds never
Gonna change.

So to the men who control this planet
Just think while you're loading your guns
That words speak louder than actions
So please put down your guns.

If all the children around
The world could all
Play together
Maybe the adults could
Learn from them
No matter what your
Colour is, we all got to heaven.

**Nikki Horton**

## A Butterfly's Day

Putting on their coloured suits,
For a day of fluttering
Showing all the pretty colours
On their big bright wings.

Flying around the flowers,
For hours they will dance
Jumping in and out of clouds
In a delicate trance.

The enormous sun welcomes them
As they fly up to her rays
They fly around and dance and glide
Like they're in a daze.

They hide in the trees
With the buzzing bees
And land on the leaves with a jump.
There wings so wide how far they glide
Through the giant sky.

**Rosie Hampshire**

## The Parting

You walked away so brave and small
With hardly a backward glance at all
And I was left already missing the hand
Which slipped into mine when we would stand
Admiring birds and worms and cats and dogs
And lorries loaded up with logs.

I walk the streets, devoid of fun
No more choosing cake or bun
No trains to watch, no ducks to feed
No racing downhill, gathering speed.
No puddles to jump, no leaves to catch
Falling from trees in a coloured patch
No more stopping to peer down holes
No more cheering when we've scored the goals.

You have no problems little man
The trouble lies here with your Gran
Who has to learn to let you go
So others can touch you and make you grow
Into a schoolboy, bright and clever
And teach you more than I could ever.

But alone, I am restless watching the clock
The slow moving hands seem to mock
My foolishness I cannot settle to any chores
But at last I can hurry to the doors
Which open on a sea of anxious faces
Scanning the throng of parents in their places
'Look Chris, there's Grandma come to collect you today'
You smile at me in your shy gentle way
Overwhelmed, I open my empty waiting arms
And you fill them again with your four-year-old charms.

**Nancy Allanson**

## Autumn Acrostic Poem

**A** hat to keep your ears warm
**U**mbrella so you don't get wet
**T**ights to keep your legs warm
**U**nder the trees collecting conkers
**M**emories of summer
**N**early Christmas!

**Asia Henshaw**

## Uncle Dumpy

Uncle Dumpy, can you tell me
Why you trash the country lanes?
With garden waste and lager tins,
And old chairs made from canes?

Instead of seeing pretty fields
And who knows? A pair of foxes!
There's ditches full of fly tipped waste
And empty burger boxes.

A mattress, ripped and full of stains -
The settee's no longer comfy.
So, out they go, just ditch them!
You're a bad man, Uncle Dumpy!

*Asbestos sheets*…I ask you -
How dangerous are they?
Just discarded in a gateway
Why? The **bad man** wouldn't pay!

'What goes around, comes around'
I believe the sayings right
I'm hoping <u>you'll</u> be dumped on soon -
*From a ruddy, great big height!*

**Sue McNeilly**

## Thirst

Walking through treasured land, yearning for a dark cloudy sky.
Tears slowly fall, and disappear by the scorching red fiery heat.
Pain mounts from head to toe, as minutes turn to hours…
Her tiny eyes gaze at a delicate sandy brown cup,
Oh how she longs for beautiful, crystal clear droplets,
Oh how she dreams for an eternity of flowing water.

Her fragile body weakens, but she fights to walk on.
Grasping her tiny ashy hands, she prays for her thirst to fade away.
Her tiny feet gradually stop as the little girl's hopes reach a stand still.
Weeping as she lays on the hot burning path,
Oh how she longs for beautiful, crystal clear droplets,
Oh how she dreams for an eternity of flowing water.

**Devina Narendra Gohil**

## The Spirit Of Nature

With sunken spirit and heavy heart, despondency grips my soul.
I just want to be still...to lick my wounds with my tears...
To be still and sense the cause that shakes my spirit
With emotions that bubble forth from the deep well of my soul.
To be still and commune with that which is of the spirit...
Of the hidden truths that surround us,
Permeating nature like a formless snake
Weaving it's way through unseen barriers in invisible dimensions
Of an ignored atmospheric communion between man and nature.
A multi dimensional world of which I am an integral part.
Desperately I seek my place in this vast invisible world of the senses...
To hear what I do not hear...see what I do not see...
Smell what I do not smell...feel what I do not feel.
To communicate and become fully attuned to the mysteries of nature.
With a hungry heart my eyes seek to feast upon the ONE
Who sits on this earthly throne of Creation?
I long to hear the beat of his heart...the pounding of his pulse...
The caress of his breathe...the healing of his spirit.
And this is where he has led me...to the silent testimony of nature,
The nature of our Divine parent...Earth Mother, Sky Father...
All that holds us in its bosom.
Our Father the cosmic sperm that initiates,
Impregnates and creates from the vast store of His infinite knowledge,
Our Mother, each one of us a cell of the Universal Child in her womb,
Joined to her life giving body by the cord that feeds us.
He has brought me here to this silent place
To be still next to her beating heart to console and comfort me...
To HEAR the sweet soothing song of her lullaby...
An orchestra of songbirds, rippling river,
wind in willows and whispering grass.
To INHALE the fragrant flowers in her hair...
taste her healing herbs...and
SEE her in the little creatures that are the aspects of her character
To FEEL safe in the arms of my dear Mother Earth
And in the Peace of my Father Sky.

**Christine Winnan**

## Let There Be Love

Let us love.
If God is good,
Let us love.
If we know what beauty is,
What we hope for, live and die for
And what makes the world go round,
If God is good,
Then let us love.

We do not need tongues
And we do not need prayer
To make the world go round.
We need the sun at our back
And the grass beneath our feet,
And we need
Friends on our hands
And magic on the tips of our fingers.

So step out the door on to the
Grass and light of today, not yesterday,
Just today and all its magic.
Take hold of me and let's see
Let's go
Let's make the world go round
Let's go
If God is good
Let's make
Glory and light and the world
Let's go
Let us say it from one end to the other
Let us love
Let there be love.

**Luke Walker**

## Night Watch

The baby's shrill screams shatter the dark silence
Like a hammer on glass.
She wakes to the sound tearing through the stillness,
And squeezes her eyes shut,
Wishing she could do the same with her ears/

Bone-weary from hours of night-walking,
Arms aching, throats dry from lullabying,
Beside her the man is still – and she is angry,
Resenting his withdrawal into exhausted sleep.

Why does he not hear the child wailing?
His child as well as hers.
How can he lie secure in some far dream world,
While screams attack her shattering her eardrums?

Reluctantly, she stumbles from her bed,
To lift again the frantic little form,
And murmur words of comfort, while her eyes
Fill with tears of weariness and frustration.

**Connie Voss**

## To My Dad

You've watched me grow from year to year
And now no doubt you shed a tear
I'm not the little girl I was
But no need to worry nothings lost.

My love for you has grown with age
And I know it will last through every stage.
I may do things you do not like
But even so you never strike.

You just sit back and grit your teeth
Mutter and moan at the end of your leash
I don't mean to do them, I just do
I'm sorry if I ever made you blue.

I love you Dad with all my heart
A love that will last even when we're apart.

**Helene Hoyle**

## Ode To Harrow-on-the-Hill

The meadow is up on the hill
The wind stirs the daffodil,
I ran up the path to the top,
When I heard the chimes of a clock,
I saw thro the trees my home,
But thought it was here I would roam.

**Margaret Heasman**

## Adieu

Don't say goodbye
Just say adieu
And don't let us leave
Feeling sad, feeling blue.
For as the seconds pass by
It gets closer to when.
We'll be smiling and hugging
And together again.

Let's not discuss
The next time we meet.
Or make any promises
That we know we won't keep.
Just say 'See you soon'
And leave it at that.
And before very long
We'll be welcoming you back.

Let us not dwell
On the day when we part.
Or let the sorrow we feel
Creep into our hearts.
Instead lets remember
The days that we've had
And of these precious times
Let us be thankful and glad.

So we won't say goodbye
We'll just say adieu
Until the next time we meet
We'll be thinking of you.

**John Rigby**

## A Sprinkle Of Magic

I feel as though some stranger,
has a desire of love and lust for me,
I feel as though this stranger,
has sprinkled magic dust on me.

Each and every speck of dust,
has brought new dreams into my eyes,
I feel as though some complete stranger,
has answered my prayers, has heard my cries.

I say it is magic dust because,
it has taught me how to smile,
I feel as though this stranger,
has gifted me with happiness for a while.

A lifetime seems to have gone by,
and all I have done is just hide away,
what is a smile, how am I meant to know,
when all my life, I have cried away.

Sprinkle some magic dust upon me,
so many tears never think of returning,
sprinkle some magic dust upon me,
so may fears turn to ashes by burning.

You came into my life as a stranger,
from a stranger you have turned to a friend and foe,
can I trust you oh stranger oh friend,
that is just something I will never know.

It you think I am special,
give me your true love and lust,
and if I am precious enough to your heart,
then gift me with some magical dust.

One sprinkle here,
and one sprinkle there,
sprinkle me, just sprinkle me
with magical dust sprinkle me everywhere.

**Salma Khan**

## Modern Love

Your imaginary arms
Circle me
And I feel safe
In your love
Secure to be me
Whole.

All that is dismal
Has gone
Forever?

Your God and
My God are one
As we were
At the beginning

How glorious
This period
While we wait
To meet our destiny

One of perfect love
And freedom
One of total trust
And compassion
One of tolerance
And obedience

The passion of life
Totally shared

Oh how I love you!

But I have to
Find you first.

**Johanna van Gorkom**

## Remember When...

Do you remember when
In those days of long ago
We danced across the ballroom floor
And went to a picture show
The organ rose majestically
It's music loud and clear
We sang the songs of yesterday
To chase the war time fear
We saw a girl across the floor
And asked for the pleasure of the dance
It was the beginning to many of us
Of a wonderful romance.
I married the girl across the floor
I see her now as I did then
The band was playing our favourite tune
Yes, I remember when.

**R Cox**

## Walking By The River

Walking by the river
On a gorgeous day
Makes my life happy
Even when as now
Things look very grey
I love my family
And I know they love me
But something is missing
And I know that always will be
The love of my life
My darling Husband
Who died three years ago
After being together
Through years of woe
Knowing him from the age of 14 years
Loving continually through the war
All I have left are memories.

**Irene Fisher**

## What Is...

What is thunder?
Someone sitting on a cloud smashing cymbals.
What is rain?
God crying.
What are hailstones?
Rabbit droppings from the sky.
Where does the wind go?
To the North Pole.
What is fog?
God dusting heaven.

**Louise Armstrong**

## A Final Dream

My nightmare, so vivid
It always seems so real
The pain that grips hold of me
Everything I feel

The drowning of my senses
The completion of the hollow
The ripping of my heart
The pity and the sorrow

Until the lights fades
And all that is left, is you
A vision of an angel
The hell I'm going through

Slowly fades and drips away
A calm I can't feel by day
I can smell your scent of heaven
I can taste you on my skin
I wont ever let this go, my dream
My unholy sin

Encasing my body, wrapping me in you
An evil soul, so perfect
For all that I go through
A haunting of my nightmares
A blessing to my dreams
Helpless to confuse me
But it shows me what I mean

The face in my reflection
Is not me, but you
a craving of one moment
to know all the things you do

Destruction of my needs
A stab of my addiction
To allow me what I want
To have the contradiction

Only for a few hours
Can I know how heaven feels
The look in eye, to hear I love you
To need and treasure
I wish it were real....

A dream is a wish your heart makes while asleep.

**Emma Rixon**

## Feather On The Floor

I found a pure white feather,
On the bedroom floor,
I looked around the bedroom,
But couldn't find no more.

An angel had paid me a visit,
That was plain to see,
Whilst I lay a sleeping,
The angel looked after me.

While I slept so soundly,
Not a pretty sight,
The angel came and guarded me,
All through the night.

I know that I'm looked after,
While I'm sleeping sound,
I can feel the angel's presence,
It's here it's all around.

I wonder will the angel
Visit me tonight,
I hope the visits will be more and more,
Lots of feathers left on the floor.

Some folks don't believe in angels,
They look after us I'm sure,
Why not look for a feather,
On your bedroom floor.

**J B Northeast**

**Seasons**

Winter smells like…
Christmas dinner with bursting crackers,
Icicles hanging down from gutters,
Silver in the moonlight.

Spring smells like…
Baby lambs and lush green grass,
Daffodils sprouting here and there,
Yellow with an orange horn.

Summer smells like…
Bunches of daisies and ruby red roses,
Sky embroidered with puffy white clouds,
Crystal clear and blue.

Autumn smells like…
Swaying trees with brown chestnuts,
Crinkly leaves, brown and crispy,
Orangey-yellow on the ground.

**Savannah Petrie**

**You**

Where do I turn when I am tired and blue? I turn to you.
Where do I go when I am sore and irritable? I turn to you.
Where do I seek respite when I am down in the dumps? I turn to you.
What do I do when all else fails? I turn to you.
What do I do when my inner sanctum desires suicide? I turn to you.
You! You! You! I turn to you.
You! You! You! I love you.

**Gary Liles**

## Instant

A road in tree shadow,
A space between pines,
A Welsh voice rising
Produce
The nuclear flash,
A world
Atomised
In an instant.
And the next,
Simply
A road in tree shadow,
A space between pines
A Welsh voice rising.

**James Kilner**

**Waiting**

I'm waiting for you Big Boy,
In the cool and icy air
Don't let me wait forever,
Let me know that you still care.

I just can't wait to see you
On this bitter night.
Can't believe you would leave me
In this lonely plight.

Maybe others need you,
Need you more than me.
Do I have to wait forever
Please listen to my plea.

If you don't get here soon
I'll go home and we will part
Never ever meet again
It's said with aching heart.

It's because I went out tonight
And tried to speak the lingo
Then tried to meet up with you
When I had finished Bingo.

Had a lovely time there,
Can't understand the fuss.
If you don't get here soon
I'll get another bus.

**Mary Hancock**

## Hands

When first we met, I soon noticed his hands.
The slender fingers, tapering at the tips, and ending
In oval shaped perfection.

They looked so elegant as they caressed
Piano keys, or held a pen.
And so they gave each movement
A meaningful and sensuous air.

I thought,
If they were mine, I'd decorate
With rings and polish of a startling hue.
I'd want to draw attention
To hands as good as those.

I'd cherish them with creams
And have expensive manicures.
Be careful not to harm
Or injure them in any way.

The opaque skin is speckled now
With age.
The veins stand proud,
The fingers slightly stiff.
His hands have changed,
But not to me.
The hands of youth,
Are still imprinted on my mind.
And there they'll stay,
For ever.

**Margaret Cross**

## Passion

Passion has abducted me,
I surrender to every request.
Touching violet lips and kissing chest.

A prisoner am I,
but not one who's scared.
Your blonde hair in my face,
my vision impaired.

Desire has owned me,
I answer only to lust.
Eyes sparkle like jewels with diamonds encrust.

A tortured soul am I,
but not one who's in pain.
Your beauty has captured me,
and my heart is slain.

Love has enveloped me,
I cannot break its seal.
Loss of dress and porcelain skin reveals.

A slave am I,
but not one who's forlorn.
Your body in my arms
to hold until dawn.

**Robert Aquaro**

## The Hedgehog

Amidst the rustic woods my winter's sleep,
awaiting springs warmth, then slowly creep.
While living that lonely quiet life,
perhaps some day find the prickly wife.

Searching the earthly floor of fallen leaves,
while listening above to the rustling trees.
Wandering about on my little feet,
maybe surprised strange ramble meet.

Searching for tasty worms under those dry leaves,
if predator near, curl up into prickly ball freeze.
But sometimes approach the roads with fear,
those terrible speeding monsters so near.

I always hope and do pray,
that I will see another day.
Because crossing roads might mean death,
I move quickly constantly out of breath.

When safe across I might secretly dance,
thank mother nature for another chance.
On some distant day I hope to have family,
with a prickly sweet wife and babies happy.

**George E Woodford**

## Halle Bopp

When I go to bed at night
I look for the comet that's large and bright
Through my binoculars I watch in awe,
To see something beautiful that's free for all.
With it's lovely tail trailing in the sky,
It brings a tear to my eye.
In the early hours when I cannot sleep,
I open the curtains to have a peep,
Yes it's still there in all its glory,
I bet Halle Bopp can tell a story
Soon it will be on its way
Going far, far away
I shall miss looking at that beautiful sight
Goodbye Halle Bopp
Large and bright
Going away into the night.

**Jean Andrews**

## The Seasons

First to awake is spring
It's such a lovely thing
Everything sweet and green
The best that's ever seen
Leaves and flowers bright and new
All in the morning dew.

Second is summer in full flow and hot
Giving everything it's got
Hedgerows and wild flowers
Honeysuckle and roses in the bowers
Sometimes, just a little rain
Making them fresh again.

Third on the scene is autumn gold
Leaves are red and brown and the wind is cold
But the colours on a lovely sunny day
Make you want to look and pray
When the sun goes down in the west
Autumn is at it's very best.

Now fourth is winter, sometimes with snow
And the clouds are very dark and low
And at it's heart is comes to pass
We all love to celebrate a Happy Christmas
Now we have nothing to fear
Because around the corner spring is here.

For all the seasons it's God we thank
It's more than gold in the bank
It's colour, beauty and love
We work with it hand in glove
It generates such a lot of power
And passes away many an hour.

**Wendy Bignell**

**Insomnia**
*(In the Nigerian Jungle)*

As I lie on my bed and I hear all around
The noise of the crickets and birds that abound
In the dark virgin jungle only God could have found,
My mind thinks of people and things far away,
Of what I'm to do and what I'm to say
To my dear ones and loved ones, when we meet one fine day.

I toss and I turn and my thoughts move again
To the time I have had in the snow and the rain;
How different out here, where the air is so warn,
Where I go to bed early and start work at dawn,
And the people are black, and I am so white,
Somehow to me it doesn't seem right!

I turn over once more, now the sweat's pouring fast.
However, I know that all this cannot last,
For all will be fresh when the morn comes again,
Like into a garden just after the rain.

My mind keeps on thinking of what I have done,
Of what I have done and those things still undone;
I should have done this and I should have done that-
Oh bother, the servant, he's drowning the cat!
Oh no, it's not, it's the birds up above,
Who never coo quietly like the pure English dove,
But they squawk and they squabble and fight all night long.
Why couldn't God give them just one little song?

My eyes become heavy, my brain becomes weak,
There's no one to love me, no one whom to speak.
The Lord has been good to me all my short life,
He's given me health, and I'm getting a wife-
So I dream of my dearest, my young wife-to-be,
And I go to sleep knowing she's thinking of me.

**Tim Brydon**

## New Life

Barely opened eyes
Unconditional trust.
No reason to be wary -
With touch as a must.

A living breathing life form
Looking from the inside out.
Will you accept me -
Or is my existence in doubt?

Reaching out for comfort
Pleased to see a friend.
A new life exposed -
From beginning to end.

What sort of life form am I
Does it really matter?
Please give me a sign -
If I need to scatter.

Are you looking after you
Enough to look after me.
What sort of life on earth -
Can I expect to see?

Half in, half out
Staring all about
It's warm and safe in here -
So, is it worth me coming out?

**Lynda Sullivan**

## Ocean Teardrops

Under a still June moon
We bound towards and jump the swell,
Cool Atlantic spray attacks a face
While the soothing night stares back,

Surf thunders down a barren swart
And the deep blue broods behind
Legs entwined, in twirling foam we lay frolicking,
There were white smiles as blinking neon found emerald eyes,

Moonlight danced on wet little legs
And rainbows played upon her hair,
That honey blizzard on beach,
The lips on that most lush,

I saw ocean teardrops lay upon her
Jewel-like sparklings shimmer,
Her body warm and slippery smooth,
She stirred with verve,

Soon there was gorgeous love on aged sands,
Touching fingertips and palms,
Slaps and sucks cried out and caught the breeze,
Wind caressed my cheeks and back,

And with a stubbly cheek along her belly
All the bleary lostness she washed away,
The boarders breached to reveal the scars
There was just silence save the gurgling waters,

Her chest? Rose gently,
She smiled at me contented; thinking her own thoughts,
While in the shadows of that mother volcano
All sorrows I consigned to the ebb and flow,

But with a caress comes the blow,
Alas' glamour turns to grey,

Now wistful memories send me to sleep
For her halcyon wings no longer beat,
There's no sweetness to shroud a muddled mind
As bitching crowds mill behind,
And that wild night sea I suffer in dreams
Foam streams - the washing white on black.

**M P M<sup>c</sup>Garrity**

## I Am

I am the child
I am the man
I am the very person that can
Be a mother
Be a son
Be a yearning for everyone
I am the sky
I am the sea
I am the very person that breathes
For every man
For every child
To be fortunate of a place in this world
I am young
I am old
I am the everlasting mould
Of the universe
Of space
Of everyone in the human race
I am...me!

**Samantha Carter**

## The Poet's Mind

Read what the Poet writes
  Hear what he has to say.
The thinking mind will tell you
  Things - that will make or break your day.

He may write about - turmoil
  War, terror, fear or strife,
Starvation and famine,
  Perhaps the - bomb - that ends all life.

It could be the blessings of nature
  As the seasons come and go,
And golden carpets of daffodils
  Maybe winters blanket of soft white snow.

Whatever he says, pray listen,
  And one day you will find,
That love, peace and goodwill,
  Are the ingredients of the Poet's mind.

**Thomas Gillen**

## The Fog Horn

On days like these when restless
I have an urge to stray
Go back to days so stress less
Those days of fun and play
When racing, panting, breathless
With sky so low and grey
We'd run the beach then reckless
Go and swim across the bay.
To the moan of the fog horn
Convention we did scorn.

Soaring like the birds of prey
High as an eagle's flight
Freedom's song to guide our way
We swam by day and night
Unfettered by social bray
We played with all our might
Games too fast for us this day
How sad our present plight.
Hear that dull, haunting fog horn
Tells of days that are gone.

With eyes that are looking back
We span the passing years
When it was all white or black
We had no doubts nor fears
To be carried in our pack
Now let us give three cheers
Brave spirit we need not lack
To face the coming spears.
To make the dismal fog horn
A fair challenge to the morn.

**William Hunt-Vincent**

## The River

In silver silence bubbling up from depths of earth,
I do not know the dark place of my birth
Or why I start this journey to the sea,
Trickling first across the grassy lea,
Then gurgling onward through the sedge,
Kingcups, buttercups fringe my silver edge.

Darting dragonflies flit overhead,
Blue reflections in my sunny, sparkling bed.
An idle brook am I with time to spare,
I take my pleasure in the scented air.
Then strong I grow and ever wide,
Through yellow gorse and thickets now I glide,
Ever dipping, rising, rushing with the rain,
Hiding deep in ferny fronds and splashing out again.

I push and carve myself a deeper bed,
Foamy wavelets forming at my head.
And on and on past rocky slopes and downs,
Through woods and copses, villages and towns.
Homes and factories wave smoke as I roll past;
I am a river, proud and flowing fast.

Then swifter still, and faster I move free.
Tossing boats towards the open sea.
My waters surge, and forth they gush,
Nothing now can halt the mighty rush.
And near the place I know I need to be
I join at last the great majestic sea.

**Barbara Keith**

## Old Boy

I'm an old boy now
And my eyes have gone dim
And I have the odd hair that grows in me chin

My legs have gone wonky
I walk with a stick
And I hear now and then but I don't miss a trick!

I'm really not 'past it' despite what you see
But I do feel more sleepy
Do you get like me?

I'll just have a catnap
And wake up refreshed
Then I'll try and remember where I put that damn vest!

I'll have a quick nibble
And maybe a wee
Then back to my chair to watch the TV

Old Age isn't that bad
It has its rewards
Like free dental check-ups - me teeth's in the drawer!

You get free prescriptions
Incontinence pads
And if you are lucky, the wretched flu jab!

I have a free bus pass
But never go out
I forget where I'm going; you should hear me shout

Yes, I'm feeling quite sleepy
Oh 'it must be my age'
I hear this so often, it does make me rage.

You wait till you're my age
Yes, you'll get there too
Where your 'forgetful' and 'senile', 'always off to the loo!'

But I do have my moments
As oft said before
But I'll mull this one over…excuse me, I snore zzz.

**Sharon Bowen**

## As The Candle Slowly Melts

I wearily close my eyes, as the darkness of night falls,
On yet another lonely day, trapped again within these walls.
I reach out to light a candle, and watch intently at its flame,
As the playful dancing light, seems to whisper out my name.

Calling me forever closer, pulling me now further in,
As I drift off to dream, from this tortured world of sin.
Consumed by the fire, releasing up my soul,
As my mind seems to wander, in a state of lost control.

In these moments of distraction, that my sanity's now dealt,
The hours pass like seconds, as the candle slowly melts.

In a corner of my mind, the distant future's what I glimpse,
Of a hell made in heaven, in a blood red rinse.
Where the angels of the devil, scream violently in pain,
Their enduring satisfaction, redeeming pleasure as their gain.

Like the decaying of a corpse, or rose petals as it wilts,
The hours pass like seconds, as the candle slowly melts.

As I see beyond illusion, reality slips in again unseen,
For these moments of gratification, alas was just a dream.
So as I struggle against temptation, self preservation's what I fight,
But this battles nearly over, and the end must fall tonight.

So as this burning mass of wax, nears the end of its belt,
My life will soon be over, as the candle slowly melts.

**Jonathan Martin**

## Life

Flowers by the roadside
Another life is lost
If only drivers cared more
And thought about the cost.

Life is very precious
We only have one chance
To have it taken from us
Without a second glance.

To lose a life this way
Must surely be a crime
So look ahead before
You cross the centre line.

Now when you're out there driving
Please take extra care
Use your mirrors keep your distance
This should safely get you there.

**Iris Wright**

## A Time Of Change
*(Albrecht Durer 1471-1528, painter, sculptor)*

Fashioning in oils on stretchered cloth,
Landscapes that graced the walls of noble German homes,
Brought to Albrecht Durer fragile fame,
The sort that matches whim and fades with passing fancy.
Prey to every newfound taste in those Renaissance years
When change was everything
And so, eclipsed by fleeting fashion
The artist turned the tools from which his talents sprang
To mound soft clay or chisel chalk and stone
Creating in more lasting form, images of such vitality
That seemed to conjure up a beating pulse
With pious prudence joined the sweeping Lutheran band
Reflecting in his work such fervency and zeal
As met the market of his time.
Now best remembered for those sculpted hands,
Which in supplication reach perhaps for recognition,
Must settle from his grave for modest mention
Which posthumous fame bestows.

**John Downer**

## Sonnet

The sirens sounded late last night at ten.
Calling and shouting to their comrades bold,
From every street there came a band of men,
Running and stumbling in the wintry cold.

The shelters underground began to fill;
The people in them sang a lilting song.
They knew the Hun had came to do them ill,
But nought could daunt that happy London throng.

The 'All Clear' sounded early in the morn;
It was the sound that they'd all waited for
And up they came again - not one forlorn -
To sleep, not dream about this cursed war.

For pilots of the R.A.F. would fight
To do the same to Germany that night!

**Daphne J Hobin**

## Ghost Orchids

In the mahogany shadows
A figure sits at a numbed desk
She thinks about Italian summers
Siberian winters and timeless rains
Imagining, at first, an
'Anywhere but here'.
Her suspicious eyes trail
To a cracked window
Then flick back again
To the tea-stained paper.
A spicy smoke slithers
To caress her scarred hand
Comforting, understanding
As ebony ink flows smoothly.
Desperately the form draws
A trio of forlorn ghost orchids.

**Leslie A Smith**

## Beauty

Is there an order to beauty?
Is it in the stars that shine above?
Or maybe in the sweet smelling rose
With it's gentle petals as they brush my skin
Or in the face of youth
That stands before a mirror
For hours on end preening and primping
The gentle flutter of eyelashes
The hair like gold so finely spun
A Botticelli angel descended from heaven.

Is it in the rain that silently falls?
Or in the gentle beat of my heart as I lie sleeping
Is it in the pain you adorn yourself with?
The warlike scars you proudly display
Or is it the smoke that curls and spins
From my burning cigarette
Catching the light, a thousand dust motes dance
I sit transfixed watching the show.

Is it in the first kiss, the rush of blood
The headiness of love, the fumbling
The furtive glances across a room
Is it in a gallery? Upon marble floors
The click clacking of shoes
As we wander from painting to painting
The quiet whispering voices that comment to each other
As we silently move from room to room.

On the stillness of a lake
I could float beneath the mist
Gazing upwards in the solitude of my mind
Be awed and silenced by the distant hum
Of the beauty all around me
In my eyes that catch each moment
My senses awakened, dancing on the air.

**Nigel Symon**

**Broken Heart**

Somehow I think I've lost my way
can barely see how I get through the day

Inside these thoughts and feelings of despair
am confused and alone and don't know how to repair

My heart has been so badly hurt
some day's it feels like it hardly works

The tears that well up in my eyes
just trying to figure out the what's and why's

As darkness falls and the night sets in
the loneliness comes and I just can't win

Tears roll down these very cheeks
night after night and week after week

Maybe sometimes I'm too hard on myself
all this sadness can't be good for my health

It's sad but true
I really do feel blue

I often wonder why was I taken for such a fool
how could someone I loved be so cruel

Looking back I should have seen
then the lies and deceit would never have been

It'll be better one day I know that for sure
and the love I feel then will be truly pure.

**Karen Gray**

## For My Son

You are our very first-born -
  The most precious you can get
Now you're about to marry -
  What do we think of that?

We've known Kate for simply ages -
  And words cannot express -
The happiness we feel for you
  We wish you all the best.

Go forth into this married life
  With love and hope and humour -
Enjoy the years that lie ahead,
  Hoping one's a baby boomer!

**Sheilagh Middleton**

## The Circle Of Life

Ten little fingers, ten little toes,
Mother's eyes and father's nose,
Where time goes no one knows,
And time goes on
Tick-tock, tick-tock.

Baby no more, an infant so cute,
A smile and a cuddle no one can refute,
And time goes on
Tick-tock, tick-tock.

School days begin with a tear and concern,
Now this small child has life to learn,
And time goes on
Tick-tock, tick-tock.

Teenage years, friends and boys,
No time now for games and toys,
And time goes on
Tick-tock, tick-tock.

Wedding rings and words 'I Do'
Two hearts as one with love so true
And time goes on
Tick-tock, tick-tock.

Now the baby's a mother, the circles complete
New hopes and new dreams lie at her feet
And time goes on
Tick-tock, tick-tock.

**Susan Lord**

## Tsunami

Heaven is very busy
The gates are open wide
A gentle voice speaks out
'You're safe now, come inside'.

Our thoughts and prayers are with them
Who suffer grief and pain
But , may the good Lord, help them
Face the future once again.
The eyes of the world are on them
There's body and soul, to heal.
'If only, if only'
it wasn't all for real.
We support our workers
Who give freely their all
There's always some one out there
To answer an urgent call
May the Spirits look down on them
Bless them, with His Grace
We are His little people
Who make up the human race.

## Dorothy Brightman

## Arthur

Our Arthur was a butcher's mate
His sausages and faggots great
His big black puddings firm and round
He sold his chitterlings by the pound
His steak and sirloin was his pride
His round of beef and silverside
Were like a picture in a frame
From near and far his custom came
His lamb it made you want to glutton
Not that old tough stuff called mutton
With new potatoes and green peas
All jaded appetites 'twould please.
His pork chops laid upon a plate
Would make you start to salivate
I heard old Mrs Price a cackling
'Hey Arthur giz a bit of cracklin'
I've seen folks marching down the street
To buy a pair of his pig's feet.
His belly draft was nice and streaky
His chickens made good Cock-a-Leekie
His ham, his liver and his pies
Were feasts set out before your eyes
His business couldn't have been better
Until one day he got a letter
It said 'Dear Arthur, you can't stay
We're going to build a motorway.

**Irene Henderson**

**Time In My Garden**

One of the nicest times of day is in the garden
Messing around, clipping, de-heading the blooms,
Weeding and then a sweep with my witch's broom.
So many glorious plants and shrubs to buy
I just chose the ones that catch my eye.
Rambling roses all over the fence,
Spreading their way along to greet the hanging baskets
And then fall onto the garden bench.
All the different shapes and sizes of garden pots spilling over the top,
They look so grand, pink, purple, yellow, white and blue,
Such an abundance of colour this is just a few,
Some of my old favourites and many are new.
I am now greeted and joined by all my furry friends,
The cats from next-door,
Misty, Amber, Smokie and Whisky, I love them all.
They come in to see us every day,
Ribbon hanging from my dressing gown on the washing line they play
Now having our dinner sat on the patio in the evening sun it makes
All the time spent working so worthwhile and fun.

**J A Blackford**

## Jubilation?
*(May 1945)*

Much jubilation
Through our nation.
Slaughter no more
The end of the war.
        But
Rations still here
Much more severe.
To pay the cost
Of many lives lost
In ships and plane
For ultimate gain
To set folk free
From tyranny.
        So
No Sunday roast
Or buttered toast.
Thick lisle hose
No kitchen rolls.
Dated fashion
Petrol ration.
Unless starlight
Pitch dark at night.
No chips or peas
Or bread or cheese.
Few eggs to boil,
No cooking oil.
No jewellery
Few cups of tea.
        Therefore
We learned to share
With love and care.

**Kathleen C White**

## Lewis

We cannot see you,
But we know you are there,
In our minds we have memories,
Which we cherish and share,
Your smile it is the sun,
That rises each and every day,
Your voice is the birds,
As they sing "come out to play,"
Your touch is the breeze,
As it gently kisses our face,
Your beauty is the flower,
With their fragrance and grace,
As it is in their beauty we see your face,
Now as darkness falls,
And the day draws to an end,
A silent prayer, kiss and hug we send,
With love we send it up above,
Twinkle, twinkle, our little star,
Watching us from afar.

**Karen Prior**

**Daytime's Dream**

The sun plumes over helmeth,
The day set fare and good,
It's gradual flooding of autumn trees
Too the crest of primrose wood.

This sight of awesome wonder
Delight's me through and through,
And colours inspire me to wonder
Can this honestly be true?

Could dreams be real at daytime light?
Do dreams really happen, only at night?
For I see sight's so glorious, I think…I may…
Go to sleep all through the night,
Then, hope to dream all through the day…

**Eric Frost**

## From A Daughter To Her Dad

I started off tiny, ever so tiny
I laughed, I cried, I gurgled and blew tiny bubbles
I gave you the biggest smile whenever you looked at me, lovingly
And when you held me so gently ever so gently - just you and me
I knew you were My Dad - the most precious person in my life
To always be there whenever I needed you .
I knew you'd never leave me.

And as I grew up, still loved and cherished
You were constantly there, still nurturing, still watching,
Still guiding and still loving
And everything was good because I knew you were My Dad.

As time went on, loves were gained and loves were lost,
But never ours
Decisions good and bad were made
And when everything seemed so bad and desolate
A brilliant light shone
But how could a light so bright ever fade?

And now presently
The light for me is as bright as it ever was
Because that light never, really faded
It was merely being looked after up above
Because you are my Dad and I am your Daughter life is good
And that's why you are still the most precious person in my life
And I love you as much as I ever have and always will

Forever and ever

Your Daughter.

**Paula Lambrenos**

## There Once Was A Man

There once was a man
Who bought a balloon
He filled it with gas
And flew up to the moon.

But when he got there
He felt all alone
So, he climbed back on board
And flew all the way home.

His friends called him silly
And they said he was daft
His reaction to this
Well, he simply laughed.

So wife and belongings
Were put on the balloon
And together they flew
Right back to the moon.

**Dieter Schafer**

## Thank You

I don't know how to thank you
for all you have done for me
but this special poem
for all the world to see
you have cared for me
and treated me
and been supportive too
A kind and compassionate person
is how I find you
several hundred people
that see you every day
I am really lucky
that you were sent my way
No words can ever thank you
but this is sent to say
I am so very grateful
for all you have done for me.

**Sue Taylor**

## The Wheelie Bin Affair

On, the bin men are a'going, they've emptied my bin.
  Each week on a Thursday it's the same bloomin' thing
They leave it 'twixt the gateposts, neither inside nor out
  And before I can retrieve it, the postman gives it a clout
He kicks it and shoves it till on its side it does lay
  But it's not his fault that the bin's in his way.
Oh, the bin men are a'coming, they're coming today
  To empty the bin in their usual way.
How I wish they'd return it to the safe, grassy ground
  In my front garden where it was found.

**Valerie Warneford**

## Now That You're Gone!

You were such a playful little cat,
Even though you were a pain you was a joy to have,
You played tricks with your friend Purdy,
Hiding, creeping, making noises in the night,
You got on so well,
And at the end of a hard day,
You would curl up on my bed together,
And sleep for what seemed to be a lifetime,
And when you woke up,
You got up to more tricks,
Chasing, rolling, pouncing on birds,
Then Purdy was gone,
You seemed so sad,
Playing on your own,
Crying, howling, looking for Purdy,
I could hardly bear it,
But then you got on with your life,
Chasing, rolling, pouncing on birds,
Sleeping on my bed,
But you got ill,
You could only eat chicken and fish,
Not yummy cat food,
You had to go for regular check ups at the vet,
You cost us a fortune with all the vet bills,
But you were worth it,
Then you stopped eating altogether,
And lost all muscle control in your neck,
Your eyes went all runny and grey,
Not like the bright orange they used to be,
Then you went to the vets,
And never came back,
You were gone.

**Charlotte Simpson**

## If Only I Could

I long to lie beneath the denim blue sky
Feel the sun kiss my eyes, my face alive
To smell the breeze that fills my lungs
Oh what it feels like to belong
If only I could.

To walk along that sandy shore
Feel the sand that I adore swirling, tickling across my feet
To watch the waves crashing leaving silver glimmers in her wake
If only I could.

To hear the lark sing her song in the early morning dawn
The rustle of the trees,
Wind gathering up all the leaves
Kids playing 'til after dark
Playful dogs barking in the park
If only I could.

If I could just sit and stare knowing I could soon be there
Stabs me like a dagger in my heart
For now I fear my end is near and soon I must depart
It eats away each new day this cancer has its hold
A few more days now 'til the end this is what I'm told
All the beauty that I see I cannot take with me
For the light draws near and I see clear
Its just not meant to be.
If only I could.

Take heed I say and fill each day
With the beauty that surrounds you
Work and play, enjoy each day live it to the full
Breathe that air, hear those sounds, the colours are like new
It's all around you just take a look
Fill your eyes and mind up good
For my last wish today will be
If only I could.

**Mary O'Brien**

## I Could Stuff A Cushion With This Lot

I could stuff a cushion with this lot, but it wouldn't be nice,
I could send it to Paris, but can't afford the price,
All sorts of rubbish, fluff and crumb,
The bag split open, the floor is a mess,
The contents of my Hoover all over my dress.

The shame of the dust, the bits and the grit,
My Neighbour will call and see every bit,
There's no room for excuses, or even a drink
What will she say, what will she think?
The dust and the paper, the toenails, the skin,
Why couldn't the dust bag just keep it all in.

I rush to the cupboard to find a new bag,
The doorbell hasn't rung; I'm really quiet glad
The times running out she'll be here before I'm done,
I told her to get here just before one,
I've found the bag but where is the ring,
I never was much good fitting this thing.

Looking down closely I see something shine,
Was that the glass mouse that used to me mine?
A tail, and an ear, but where is the head?
I bought it in Brighton, with my first husband Fred,
That was a great time, we laughed on the pier,
Oh what am I doing, my neighbour is here.

It's all right Janet; please step over the mess,
And please excuse the state of my dress,
I wanted it perfect I wanted it nice,
It's no good when your Hoover eats broken up mice,
I'm sorry you've seen it, but what can I say?
I didn't know the Hoover bag would burst today!

**Denise Sheppard**

## I Am Doomed For Life To Be Without A Boyfriend

I am never going to get a boyfriend in my life.
Do I have to go through all my life without a man?
Why?
Can't I get beyond fancying an odd man?
How many more years do I have to keep hoping and
Praying it may get closer to a relationship?
My prayers are going none stop to
God Angels Spirit Guides and Spirits.
Is this how I am going to have to spend the rest of my life?
What is wrong with me I keep asking over and over again?
What is wrong?
I don't know/
I don't know why I have no man in my life.
I am not getting any answers.
I never do.
It is not for the want of wanting.
I do want a descent man in my life the right man.
What is it that is making me so undesirable to men?
I am beginning to think I have had a curse put on me.
Whose put it there and why?
How do I get uncursed?
I am doomed for life to have no boyfriend.
It keeps hurting me very much inside.
My tears are constantly flowing are very painful.
It is so obvious to me,
Somewhere there is something wrong.
Where is it I don't know?
I wish I did
Come on tell me. Tell me. Tell me please.
Where do I go who can I seek to ask?

**Jenifer Ellen Austin**

## Thank You

Thank you for things that complete your life,
A friend or relative, husband or wife.
For the love and the comfort that covers the strife.
Thank you for nature, but not for the greed,
Thanks for the bread on which we feed.
Thanks for equality, making things fair.
Thank you God for letting us share,
Creating the world and showing you care.

**Vicky Bartlett**

## Alone

Although she is never much on her own
She is surrounded by people never alone
She knows that they all really care
Family around her everywhere
But what they don't see is in her heart
That breaks each day and is torn apart.

Although she is never much on her own
She is surrounded by people but always alone
Day by day her life goes by
Nothing much happens they don't see her cry
Sometimes her loneliness is very hard to bear
Circumstances she cannot change so she stays here.

Although she is never much on her own
She is surrounded by people never alone
Each day becomes the same as the one before
With dreams that will stay outside her front door
Beyond her reach may live the love she needs
Nothing can or will change no matter how much she pleads.

Although she is never much on her own
She is surrounded by people never alone
Each day she sets her mind elsewhere
No one would know she has a care
She waits for the quite moments in her day
To cry alone, gently wiping the tears away.

**Marie Gibney**

## The Traveller

Many miles I have travelled in my time,
Lots of places I've been and seen.
And lots of friendly faces I've left behind,
But still lots of places I've not yet been,
Only seen in dreams.
Travelled down many motorways and country lanes.
Seen lots of rivers, pretty lakes and streams.
Crossed the land by car, train, foot or plane.
Through all kinds of weather,
Snow, hail, thunder and rain.
Places that have been quiet or rowdy.
Some places I never wish to see again.
Plenty to see or do.
A walk around where historic buildings remain.
Villages, cities and towns, I can't remember their names.
Nightlife, people, lights and sounds.
But even when I'm travelling,
Home is where my heart can be found.

**Anna Taylor**

**Inch**

The beach at Inch is endless sand
And the mountains sweep down to the sea,
This is my paradise and always will be.
The sea-spray like foaming fountains
Leaps to meet the awesome mountains.
As I walk, the white-capped rollers crash
                                        upon the golden strand.

Before my last breath, before my eyes close
                                        in final sleep
what shall I see?
Where shall I be?
In paradise, on my beloved Inch strand.
Scatter my ashes there 'tween mountains and sea
That I may rest eternally where the rollers swirl and leap.

**Ruth Berry**

## Scrub A Dub Dub

Scrub a dub dub
I'm in the tub but I don't
Like it anymore
The water is too cold
The soap is too old
Get me out of here.

**Bryony Llewellyn**

## Memories

An old man laughed,
as he had once done as a child.
with a ray of sunshine in his eyes,
playing in a field of memories.
as he travelled back through time,
back to a place he felt safe,
back to a place were life was simple.
not like a grown man who is afraid to cry,
but a child who is afraid of nothing.
no troubles.
no worries.
life was perfect,
for a little boy,
who has now grown old.
nothing left in his life,
but memories dancing around inside his head.
no home to go back to,
but memories he clings to like a child his father.
memories of a happy young boy.
these are the memories that made him laugh,
these are the memories that kept him alive.
with a ray of sunshine in his eyes,
and a smile upon his face,
he goes to sleep with happy memories of childhood.
never to be sad again.
from his happy dreams
he shall never wake.

**Charlotte Hargreaves**

## After All, It's Only Just A Word!

When something is out of reach
and far away you feel like giving up,
yet as years filter through,
life changes,

you grow, develop and sustain.

When something so powerful enters
an empty shell,
it grows and manifests itself
into a desired effect rarely felt

in this confused and angry world.

When compassion is no longer something
but the absolute truth,
the fervour and veracity combined
increase understanding so real

it takes two.

When two know each other
so well, nothing in the world
can tear them apart
they grow with essence and compatibility so unique

they transpire accomplishment.

**Simon Pope**

## Unrealistic

A box of chocolates in which we ate,
An extra pound on my weight,
A ring from him that I wore,
It disappeared to the back of the draw.
A single rose to keep on my bedside,
Two weeks later and then it died.
A message from him 'I Love You'
You reply I love you too.
Not much later he's gone away,
After he promised he's here to stay
An empty feeling, abandoned and alone,
If only before you met him you would've known.

**Amanda Carrington**

## Endearment

My little opiate vial.
My little razor'd apple.
My little ink'd needle.

My little back-alley dice.
My little bag of mirror shards.
My little pool of male tears.

My little fruit of Eve.
My little piano wire.
My little bloody crusade.

Dreams, pain, commitment.
Hope, fear, weakness.
Desire, anger, sacrifice.

**Matthew Long**

**Today**

Do something remarkable.
Do something amazing today.
Who does?
Who does, but doesn't know they have?
Change your life as often as you change your mind,
Change your socks.
We are all there, but never here.
If you disappeared would anyone even notice?
Would the newspapers and milk bottles pile up on the doorstep?
Don't let loneliness be your legacy.
Touch just two people in your life.
That's enough.

**Lorraine Martin**

## There Is A Place In Heaven
*(Dedicated to my friend, Elsie)*

There is a place in heaven,
Where all good people (and animals) go,
It must be a bit like Devon,
And hardly ever has snow.
The sun shines and the sea is blue,
And there's ever so much for you to do.
You can meet with your mates,
Or go on dates (if you're single),
See your mum and dad
And never be sad.
Meet with your sisters and brothers,
Aunts, Uncles and all the others.
It must be a wonderful place,
Because He sometimes makes it a race,
To take family and friends.
But he often sends,
A replacement to ease the strife,
In the form of a new life.
A baby so pink and so sweet,
And the circle of life is complete.
Heaven must be a wonderful place,
It contains the whole Human Race.

**Anthea Hurst**

**My Pop**
*(With love always)*

When I was a little girl
No longer they could wait
They took you up to heaven
And opened up that gate.

I can't remember much
As I was only three
But I will always hate
That day you went from me.

I know you're looking down on me
I often feel you near
Sometimes I wander what you were like
It makes me shed a tear.

I wonder if you're sitting here
Beside me on my bed
Telling me to go to sleep
Lie down and rest my head.

In many years to come
When my life comes to a stop
I hope to see you at the gate
I love you so much, Pop.

**Vikki Edgar**

## Love

Love, oh my love, why do you grow
Are you from the heart, or from the very soul
Are you there in a kiss, or there from the start
Just waiting to reveal, just what's in our heart?

Are you like a spirit, caught in the breeze,
What do you feel, and what do you see,
Are you a feeling, or are you much, much more,
The very keys, to our soul and its door...

Do you hide away, from the nature of man,
To reveal all your glory, like only you can.
In times of trouble, to show us the way,
To bring us new hope, and brighten our day...

Are you more than just feelings, a person inside,
Our hidden spirits, from whom we cannot hide,
So why do we fear you, or not let you grow
To make the world better, isn't that so?

My love, oh my spirit, I now ask you to be,
Let me feel what you feel, and see what you see,
To make life have meaning, to always be true,
So let me see what you see, let me be you...

**Gary Edwards**

**The Coat**

It was in a charity shop window on a tailors dummy posing.
For three days it had stood there, each day, more disarming.
The more I looked the more I liked, the more I felt we suited,
And when eventually I went in, my change tin I had looted.

That coat was black and long…and new, or so it seemed to me,
The only way to really make sure was to go inside and see.
So in I went upon my mission, to interview the coat
And if we liked each other, maybe it would just work out

The assistant smiled and said 'How can I help you today',
Pointing to the coat I said 'May I', 'Of course you may'.
Off to the changing room went that coat and I, together,
And then I saw the price and size, FOURTEEN, 'Oh bother',

In the last few months I've lost some weight, two sizes actually,
From a size twenty to sixteen, but will it be enough, we will see.
Off with the old and on with the new, I hold my breath and pray,
But when I look it fits, 'Thank you God you made my day'.

I can see you have not travelled far but what I cannot understand,
Is why anyone with any sense would make you second hand.
Your quality is of the best and your fabric is the finest,
 I'm sure we will deal very well; let's go home your highness.

As I stepped out from the changing room the assistant smiled…again.
'Is everything ok' she asked 'Oh yes just great' I said
'It's a lovely coat really smart and it suits you down to the ground'.
It is almost was down to the ground… But I smiled
And I gave her my fifteen pounds.

**Kathleen Paddon**

## I've Broken The Cycle

I've broken the cycle, broken the curse,
My life from now will get no worse,
Out of ashes I emerge stronger,
Never again will he do me wrong,
I am a phoenix, and now I will fly,
They will hurt me no more, however they try,
No more tears and no more pain,
Never again will my life be the same,
I'm stronger now and I have won,
Its time for me to live in the sun.

**Nikki Long**

## Nightmares In My Shadows

Pondering about the dream,
Wondering upon the wall,
Have you ever seen such a thing at all?
Peering out your eye,
Gazing into the nights sky,
Imagining a creature,
Who's just flown by,
Think of the worst you can,
What might this be?
Spiders, teeth and claws,
These are fears that walk upon me,
What is the worst?
What could these do?
Inflict pain or kill you,
You try to sleep, peace,
Hoping for silence,
But appears a bang,
So you awake,
Shadows creep across the floor,
Something appears behind your door,
Instant image of fears,
Not really thinking of what is meant,
Staring at the carpet,
Throwing teddies to the floor,
Finding nothing is behind my door,
Just in my mind,
This is a relief,
And slowly I drift back to sleep.

## Sharnie Healey

## I Used To Think

I used to think I could do anything,
As long as there was a smile upon my face.
And yet sometimes I used to think,
My heart was in the right place.
But then my life turned upside down,
That gleaming smile turned into a frown.
That life I'd loved,
And now I fear
Is this my life?
Filled with sorrow and tears.
But the smiles came back,
With the help of some friends.
Just knowing they care is great,
And knowing their loyalty to you never ends.
This world of frowning faces,
Is not easy to overcome,
Alone you can't,
But together as one.
I found a way with the help of my friends and so will you,
Together you will find the strength to carry on.
I know I did,
Because I told on them so it wouldn't go on eternally,
I did something about it.
I nipped it in the butt,
Before the butt nipped me.

**Natassia Caitlan Cole**

## Agony And Casualty

Seven hours approximately the agony awaits
To see a fine nurse mending the hurt
Wrapping and strapping the emergency case.

Vending machine is out of order
There's one beyond the fracture corridor
X-rays show from head to toe
The plaster is ready and seven hours to go.

Doctors in green all sterilised and clean
Examine casualties who become pretty mean
Reception calls another name
The wheelchair is brought up to help the lame.

First on the list went to the end
A punk and a drunk go to the front
Casualties' appalled security was called
And put to the end was the drunk and the punk
Seven hours is the waiting time.

Down the corridor was in an uproar
The bedpan was spilt all over the floor
A man in a crutch went to complain
The nurse threw a fit and got the blame.

My seven hours is up I have to go
Take my seat and watch the show.

**Patricia Bennett**

## Twilight Walk

When darkness streaks across the sky
And colours change to muted greys
And distant rain-clouds ride the hills
As nature's kaleidoscope displays
The symphony of early night
And silhouetted birds in flight
Their distant cries echoing still
I stand and watch their wings, until
The very last is lost to sight.
Heralding approaching night;

And in that most exquisite space
Through and around my trees, I trace
That wondrous pathway, worn in youth
When all I knew was love and truth
And wandered freely, free from fear
That there was any danger near,
For when among creation's bloom
What reason should I fear the gloom?

**Alison Siwek**

## Conversation With My Father

Life should be a laugh, but not a joke,
Yet there can be no laughter without tears
No ups without downs
No love without grief,
No winners without losers,
There can be no escape from eternity
Only surrender to its rule
Wisdom is not achieved in acquiring this truth
But achieving peace of mind by accepting it

**Alexander Prosper**

## Eire

The moon perpetually watches upon her vast green fields.
The sun warms her heart to the core of her very being.
The rain caresses and encourages her earthy body.
She dutifully gives birth to crops a plenty.
Man becomes hypnotised,
Enslaved he works only for his enchanting queen.
The collective Irish memory holds the key of understanding

Fairy rings aimlessly scatter across her impressive landscape.
Rivers and streams compliment her voluptuous hills and valleys.
Haunting melodies, steeped in tradition echo through the misty air.
Men march in unison to defend her every honour.
The collective Irish memory holds the key of understanding.

Death casts an eerie shadow on her evergreen coat.
Her streams and rivers flow deep crimson.
Her tears of sorrow flood the divided land.
She wails, a doomed banshee.
The collective Irish memory holds the key of understanding.

The fairy rings now lie desecrated.
Her body has been ravished, stripped of all its glory.
She lies helpless, exposed to the harsh winds of time.
Man has betrayed her trust, as a loving mother she awaits his return.
The collective Irish memory holds the key of understanding.

## Sharon Pickering

## Don't Wake My Guardian Angel

My husbands gone and left me - left me all alone.
My pride and joy he took with him even in my home,
The dust it gathers round me - it starts to pile high
And all I do is glance at it - glance at it and cry.
I think that soon I'll join him, join him in the ground
For since he went and left me no happiness I've found.
I have a guardian angel that came to visit me
One day when it was raining I found her in the weeds.
I gave her sips of water - a little piece of fish.
Someone to care for us. We have a common wish.
Don't wake my guardian angel - she's sleeping on the mat.
Don't wake my guardian angel - my own beloved cat.
My home's regained its sparkle my face is shining too.
A simple little creature has brought me smiling through.

**M Clark**

## Walled Garden

From within the haze
I find myself entombed
In a wonderful world,
The scene of what
Can be, more so,
What will be
A heartfelt haven.

My senses are sweet-scented
As this Eden is heaven,
The allure to me
Was far too strong,
I enchant myself in
This protected sanctuary.

when life is full
the seasons saturate
This sanctity,
My back is now against a wall.

Weathered, cold, deepening haunt,
Towering progenetor protector
Thwarts my benign adversity.

Clouding, darkening dream
Left distant and direful,
Roses rise yet with
dogmatic thorns that
Shield and fortify sanity.

A mode unsafe to enter
Until the walls crumble with time,
Recanting of last season,
But re-rooting the foundation,
to replenish a garden of virtue
that is you...

**Peter Murray**

## Moment In Time

Running from time,
A man pays for peace,
In honesty or a golden feast,

A self war of hate,
Self imaged fate,
Seizes the moment in glory,
To tell his life story,

A tale to tell
Into paradise from hell
The sun burns a ray,

Lights a fire to desire,
Bottom to top and higher,
Broken face turns the card to face,
An ace to grace.

**Paul Billett**

## My Lovely Girl

My girl sits on our garden seat
So beautiful, so trim, so neat
She is a vision to behold
There's no one like her
So I'm told
Her face and smile beyond compare
As are her nails - and her hair
Her luscious lips are so divine
I love to put them close to mine
Her deep blue eyes
So clear and bright
Makes my world a shining light
She is divine - you'd think so too
If you loved her like I do
I can hold her - love her dear
And she loves me - that's clear
She has a classic name - Elaine
But she's only made of Porcelain

**Martin Selwood**

## Murky Waters

Shallow water
Seems so deep
When your feet
Won't reach
The bottom.
Fears drown
Your thoughts
And pull you under
Into sweet oblivion.
It's safe
Down there,
Even though
You struggle
For breath.

In the depths
And darkness
Lies security.
No need
To be afraid
When your fears
Can only descend.
But in those
Murky waters,
No one
Can hear
You scream.
So swim back up
To the surface.

**Emma Jaques**

## For My Eyes Only

As I open the window what can I see
The tree is full of blossom from the apple tree.
The water feature bubbles like a little brook.
The birds are flying down there just to have a look.
The bluebells sway in the gentle breeze.
Daffodils bend as upon their knees.
No time to stop at the start of day.
Close the up the window as I start another day.

**Maggie Lewis**

**The Fear Within**

Driven to extremes by twisted roads that lie ahead
Every corner uncovers the deepest fear within
I hold my breath deep within my chest
While my heart plays with its own rhythm
Dancing with each pained heart beat
Till the fear inside dissolves into a twisted violent purple sky.

The soul within drives you speeding throughout life
Among a world full of bleeding hearts
Influences of danger and destruction standing proud
Sensations surround the curvatures of the body
Which throb with uncontrollable urges and desires
Deep holes of life embed each person with the fears within.

**Emma Louise Brown**

## Little Poddington-by-the-Sea

In Little Poddington-by-the-Sea
Everything stops at five for tea.
Hot toasted crumpets with strawberry jam.
Triangular sandwiches (pickle and ham).
Peaches and cream, custard and jelly,
Something good to watch on the telly.
At five of the clock the best place to be
Is Little Poddington-by-the-Sea

**David Hern**

**Dark Dream**

He jumped, and skipped, and twirled the Pygmy
As he made his way to the cold, and dripping Nymph
Her dress hung with glitter of oyster, barnacle and cyst.

He took her hand and to the dance-floor, a sty
As numerous odours surround him, like deaths myrrh
Her genteel, rocking to and fro, like the sea, gave easy rhythm.

He sang and whispered in her ear black and devilish hymn
As her mind; pictured the dark and eerie myth
Her quests, like mad-dogs possessed, gyrate and there create a gym.

He as her and I Odysseus conversed with phantoms in Styx.

**John Fearon**

## A Dockside Tavern

In a Dockside Tavern
A drunken sailor tried to sell his shoes
'Get out of here' the landlord roared
'No more booze for you'.
A spindly lass nicknamed Betty Drainpipe
Because she was so thin
Slowly tottered to the bar
To swig another gin.
Then little Ted the landlord's son
Did a frantic clog dance with
A pint upon his head.
A one armed man began to sing
'I'll take you home again, Kathleen'.
And a toothless Irishman joined in with
'The wearing of the green'.
Good times Girls sit with painted lips
Out smiling one another
There is bound to be a catfight
Before the night is over
I still see them all in my minds eye
In that smoky pub of days gone by.

**Jean Sutton**

## My Secret Love
*(For Bronwen)*

Your eyes are green, your hair is brown, your lips as red as wine,
The first time when I saw you, I wished that you were mine.
The way you took my outstretched hand, as gentle as a dove,
You thrilled my sad and lonely heart; here's some one I could love.

Secretly I watched you grow to womanhood from youth,
I never let my feelings show, I hid from you the truth.
The truth is that I love you, like no one else before,
Fulfilling all my wildest dreams - you only I adore.

My heart cried out for love and warmth, denied me many years.
So many hopes had foundered in misery and tears.
But this time it is different, for you whom I adore -
Must never know my secret, this love for you I store.

I love you more and more each day, but I must never show
To you or to the outside world, this happiness I know.
Some day you'll find your true love, who'll sweep you off your feet
Believe me dear; you'll know it, the moment when you meet.

You'll see some one across a room, when Cupid's arrow flies
A light you've never known before, shining in his eyes.
So don't delay, make sure my dear, claim him for your own;
If he loves you, as I do, you'll never walk alone.

**Frank Johnson**

## Never Alone

If we can imagine,
That time stood still.
Would you swim the deepest river?
Would you climb the highest hill?

Would you kiss the one you cherish?
Would you hold a babe in arms?
Would you wonder at your surroundings?
In a world still and calm.

Would you walk silently through soaken streets?
And dare to jump in puddles.
No-ones looking, no one cares,
They're all silent to your troubles.

Would your smile cross your face?
Where pain used to lie,
Would you banish all your worries,
And sit gently down and cry.

Would you feel lonely with out people?
Who are constant at your side?
Do you long to join life's merry go round,
In case you miss the ride.

You hope the clock starts ticking,
So normality is regained,
You realise in your silence,
It's your world that makes you sane.

Your happiness is vital,
With out it time stands still,
You're the warmth in our fire,
Your clock starts ticking because you're REAL!

## Michelle Bates

## Grief

The only time we didn't kiss
Or say goodbye take care.
You hurried out in such a rush
No time I thought to spare.

Meet me after work you said
The local
Then you went
I never saw you after that
Till lying so content.

The call it came at quarter to one
Was meeting you at two
The voice just said I have bad news
My darling it was you.

If only I had kissed goodbye
Or even said take care
I wasn't even with you
I wish I had been there
I wish so many things my dear
This life it's just not fair.

**Linda Lester**

## Natural Drama

The cat moves oh so stealthily
Towards the thick green bush
A bird is feeding hungrily
I think it is a thrush
So unaware of danger
It must have young to feed
I see it tugging at a worm
Part hidden by a weed
The cat moves ever closer
It's belly to the ground
I feel a tingle to my skin
My heart begins to pound
The cat takes off
I shout out loud!
The bird let's go its prey
And in an instant it's airborne
And well out of harms way.

**Bob Oliver**

## Be This A Dream

Be this a dream
Then may I sleep
Forever in my present life
For if I wake
And you're not there
I could not live without my wife.

If this is now
May I stay awake
To share the time with you my wife
For if I sleep
Then just to dream
Would seem as naught to actual life.

**Ray Ryan**

## You Are Everything A Father Should Be

You are everything to me,
Everything a father should be.
I know you're not my real dad,
When you came in to my life, I was glad.

Until I found you, I was all for my mother,
Clinging to her as I felt insecure with any other.
You built up my trust, showing me you weren't like the rest,
For that I will always respect you you're the best.

You make me feel safe whenever you are near,
Comforting me when I shed a tear.
I, like other people have memories that will never disappear,
Some are good, some are bad, from things we see and hear.

Before you came into my life, I felt a little rejected,
I can honestly say that I have been affected.
Then I look around and see you standing there,
It makes me realise that you really do care.

As long as you are here teaching me right from wrong,
Teaching me how to be strong.
Showing me affection, in the best way you can,
I know like you, I'll grow into a fine young man.

I feel so proud when I think back to the day
you took me on as your son,
I want to thank you for every thing you have done,
I will make it up to you some day, just you wait,
As you are my father and my number one mate.

**Kym Marie Forth**

## Grandfather

A candle burning on a windowsill,
His eyes glanced up like marbles,
His shoulders bore the weight of the world.

His body was frail and broken,
But his mind was kept intact,
He couldn't remember the last time
He saw a ray if light on a cloudy day.

His voice was cracked and old, rugged like a diamond
But when he spoke
It was like crystal water dripping through your ears.

His smile broke a thousand worries,
My dreams shattered and fell to the cold hard ground, reality
I would never see that smile again
He closed his eyes and breathed through
whatever part of his lungs the cancer hadn't taken.

When he breathed, his life, his hopes escaped and lead him to heaven.
Death took him as he breathed his last breath.
It started to rain.
And the candle was extinguished.

**Kate Hyatt**

## Niggles

Started to doubt you, but I will never know why,
Dreadful thoughts filled my mind and I started to cry.
I could not bear it if you said we must part,
Would certainly be reason of my broken heart.

Tried to put the niggles to the back of my mind,
Put on an act, fooled people for most of the time.
Although sometimes my rigid composure would slip,
Then I would be seen with a tear and bitten lip.

But you came to visit, put everything right,
After broken nights sleep, I must have looked a fright.
You saw beyond the superficial, loudly joked,
That if you seemed off with me, then you were provoked.

This said with long laugh and large twinkle in your eye,
And which immediately made me start to cry.

**S Mullinger**

## Abandoned

I'm lying on a bed kicking my heels.
Strapped tightly down, how frightening it feels.
I saw a man in gown and mask of green;
He is the strangest man I've ever seen.

He presses something soft against my face
and I begin to feel my senses race.
My world explodes with stars, I spiral down
into a tunnel where I'll surely drown.

Then I awaken to a threatening gloom;
See shadows lurking in a darkened room.
Strange ladies flitting by, in caps of white,
on soft soled shoes as quiet as the night.

All around me little children cry, and I am
crying too as in my bed I lie.
I twist and turn and whisper with a groan
'If my mum loves me why am I alone?'

**Maureen Edden**

## Purely Private

Essence of presence, our right to defend
Sacred sanctity, the private domain
Scientific technologies strain,
Life itself becomes a product to vend.

The wooded eaves creek, the light starts to leak,
Land sun intrudes and always achieves
Nature's evolution, the web that weaves
The threads of life so delicately deep.

There I sit like china upon my seat.
Close to the edge the floating globe transits.
Cool to the eye as the tocked-ticks creep,
The destiny of humanity twists
With subtle sophisticated technique,
Our own intelligence is now a risk.

**Rebecca Fludgate**